HAL•LEONARD
INSTRUMENTAL
PLAY-ALONG

AUDIO ACCESS INCLUDED

QUEEN

UPDATED EDITION

PLAYBACK+
Speed • Pitch • Balance • Loop

To access audio visit:
www.halleonard.com/mylibrary

Enter Code
1562-2711-6616-2942

© Jorgen Angel/CTSIMAGES
Audio arrangements by Peter Deneff

ISBN 978-1-5400-3846-3

HAL•LEONARD®

Visit Hal Leonard Online at
www.halleonard.com

Contact Us:
Hal Leonard
7777 West Bluemound Road
Milwaukee, WI 53213
Email: info@halleonard.com

In Europe contact:
Hal Leonard Europe Limited
42 Wigmore Street
Marylebone, London, W1U 2RN
Email: info@halleonardeurope.com

In Australia contact:
Hal Leonard Australia Pty. Ltd.
4 Lentara Court
Cheltenham, Victoria, 3192 Australia
Email: info@halleonard.com.au

ANOTHER ONE BITES THE DUST

VIOLA

Words and Music by
JOHN DEACON

CRAZY LITTLE THING CALLED LOVE

VIOLA

Words and Music by
FREDDIE MERCURY

BICYCLE RACE

VIOLA

Words and Music by
FREDDIE MERCURY

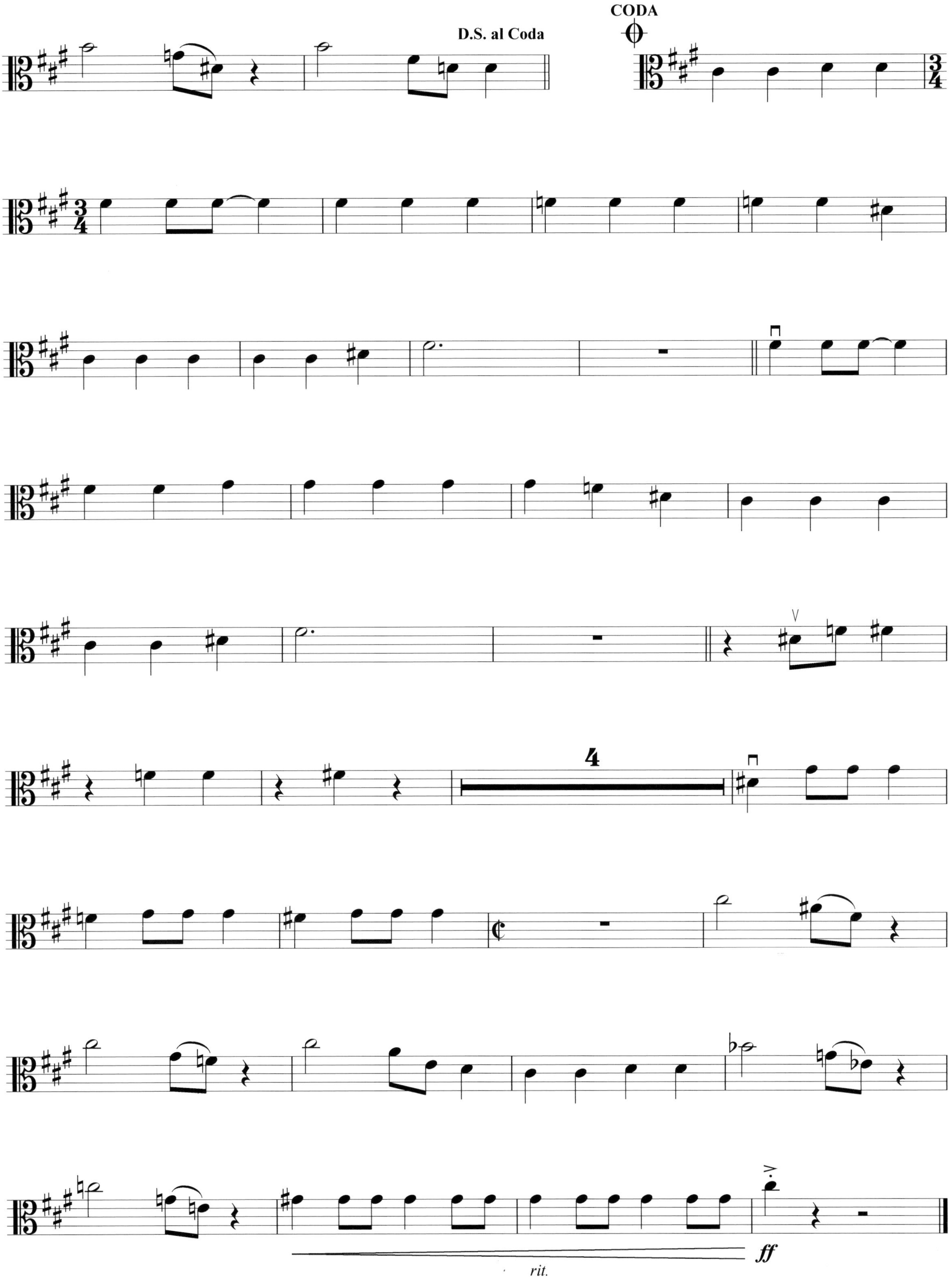
D.S. al Coda
CODA
4
rit.
ff

BOHEMIAN RHAPSODY

VIOLA

Words and Music by
FREDDIE MERCURY

Hard Rock Shuffle
4
f
3
molto rit.
Slow Rock
mf
2
mp
rit.
4
p

FAT BOTTOMED GIRLS

VIOLA

Words and Music by
BRIAN MAY

I WANT IT ALL

VIOLA

Words and Music by FREDDIE MERCURY,
BRIAN MAY, ROGER TAYLOR
and JOHN DEACON

DON'T STOP ME NOW

VIOLA

Words and Music by
FREDDIE MERCURY

f
D.S. al Coda
CODA

I WANT TO BREAK FREE

VIOLA

Words and Music by
JOHN DEACON

PLAY THE GAME

VIOLA

Words and Music by
FREDDIE MERCURY

KILLER QUEEN

VIOLA

Words and Music by
FREDDIE MERCURY

mf
2
D.S. al Coda
CODA
mf
f
mf
2

RADIO GA GA

VIOLA

Words and Music by
ROGER TAYLOR

SAVE ME

VIOLA

Words and Music by
BRIAN MAY

SOMEBODY TO LOVE

VIOLA

Words and Music by
FREDDIE MERCURY

f
D.S. al Coda
CODA

UNDER PRESSURE

VIOLA

Words and Music by FREDDIE MERCURY,
JOHN DEACON, BRIAN MAY,
ROGER TAYLOR and DAVID BOWIE

f
mf
mp
p
4

WE ARE THE CHAMPIONS

VIOLA

Words and Music by
FREDDIE MERCURY

WE WILL ROCK YOU

VIOLA

Words and Music by
BRIAN MAY

YOU'RE MY BEST FRIEND

VIOLA

Words and Music by
JOHN DEACON